Watched

Watched

Poems

David Paul Folyant

The Hermit Kingdom Press
Cheltenham ★ Seoul ★ Bangalore ★ Cebu

WATCHED: POEMS

Copyright © 2004 by David Paul Folyant

All rights reserved. No part of this book may be reproduced in any form or by any means, electronic or mechanical, including photocopying, recording, or by any information storage and retrieval system, without permission in writing from the publisher.

ISBN 1-59689-001-0

Write-To Address:

The Hermit Kingdom Press
3741 Walnut Street, Suite 407
Philadelphia, PA 19104
United States of America

Info@TheHermitKingdomPress.com

Hermit Kingdom
12 South Bridge, Suite 370
Edinburgh, EH1 1DD
Scotland

http://www.TheHermitKingdomPress.com

For all who are watched but persevere

POEMS

watched
11

the fear factor
13

walking camera
16

like a london bus
18

who?
20

empty it's not
22

pretty flowers there
24

i look and look
26

advantage
28

exploitation
30

approval
32

insider trading
34

abused
36

i am deprived
38

hearts have become hardened
41

the evil game
43

a teacher without pay
45

easy to sabotage
47

being watched
49

Watched

watched

i sit here and know
that i am
watched

like a fish swimming
in a rectangular tank
transparent glass

on all sides
visible from every
angle

every stroke of computer
key
that i push

each blink
wink
and twitch

i am watched
like a fish
inside a rectangular tank

the world isn't round
with endless possibilities to
explore

there are walls
on all sides
with my every motion monitored

the fear factor

it is because they are
afraid
that they watch

thinking that they can
fathom
the mind

the prediction of the future
to know how to grasp the reality
modify to fix things

the fear factor
being afraid of the future
what might happen

they watch
with contentment
thinking they can change

their destiny
written in the stars
still hidden in nature's mystery

they watch
thinking they can control
everything

including the future
life
world

Watched

everyone
in the world
companies

individuals
alike
together

they think they can control
if they only could see
if they could always know

they act
because they are afraid
they watch

because of the fear
that grips their very being
they know

they are afraid
even though they try to deceive
themselves

they know deep down
they watch because of fear
and feel more and more uncertain

with each
advancing
day

Watched

walking camera

walking camera follows me
everywhere i go
like a shadow
that can't be separated

like a novice reporter
trying to prove her worth
the camera follows me
to prove something

even before i move
the moving camera
tries to anticipate
my move

the invisible camera
walking silently behind
tries to walk before me
to show me that it knows

the walking camera
has grown proud
like a human being who experienced
too many victories

now it can't help itself
but to show that
it knows
that it can even predict

like a london bus

i am like
a london bus
big and resolute
driving with confidence

like a london bus
I am hard to capture
for i move fast
avoiding to speed

like the naked eye
following the london bus
the camera follows me
trying to keep up

to be placed to capture
my scene
even as i speed
down the london street

i am to be captured
my image to be made available
to be seen
publicly like the london bus

i drive recklessly
like the london bus down
strand
to elude the traffic

but
alas
i am pictured
by the speeding camera

Watched

who?

who is interested?
who has something to gain?
why am i watched?

do they want my knowledge
free of charge?
to enslave my mind for their profit?

why am i being watched?
who has a vested interest
in watching me?

to read
everything
that i write

simultaneously
as my pen
touches the paper

to watch
all
that i read

as my eyes
follow the letters
on the pages of the book

who wants to see?
what has he to gain?
at the expense of whom?

empty it's not

it looks empty
but it is not
there is someone watching

through the camera
placed there
especially for me

they watch
with a particular purpose
to gain something from the view

and let others watch
to cover their tracks
their sinister intentions

empty it is not
even if the whole room is empty of people
the camera is there

i am watched
by the evil ones
who want to gain

and they drag others in
to cover their evil intent
to get all involved

Watched

pretty flowers there

there are pretty flowers there
and i think to myself
how pretty they are

i stand to watch
their pretty colors
and feel special

thinking i am alone
in private
together with the pretty flowers

pretty flowers there
they are so pretty
prettier than any i have ever seen before

and i feel fortunate
that i am here
with pretty flowers there

alone
special
in private

then i realize
i am not alone
i am being watched

Watched

i look and look

i look and look
but i don't see the camera
or many cameras
they capture my presence

my movement
motion
gesture
expression

captured for the screen
to be seen
from every angle
frozen in time

but i don't see
where the cameras are
they are there
but where are they?

who placed the cameras there?
how did they get in here?
who gave whom authorization?
where are the damn cameras?

advantage

do you not think
they will use
what they see
to their advantage?

i am being watched
they see
they know
weaknesses and strengths

don't you think
they will abuse their knowledge
unfairly gained
to their advantage?

it is human nature
to abuse information
in competition
you know

don't you think they will use
unfairly gained info
to beat me
unfairly in a competition?

exploitation

it is exploitation
unjust
and unethical
unfair

to watch me
my every move
without my consent
without asking me

then to use the information
against me
like you are righteous
as if you have done nothing wrong

it was exploitation
it is exploitation
it will be exploitation
what you do

to watch me
without my consent
like you own rights to me
but you don't

yet you go on
exploiting
participating in exploitation
approving exploitation

approval

will you continue
to give your
approval?

as i am exploited
by the many cameras
placed here

without my consent
against my will
dehumanizing me

they do wrong
unethical work of slavery
using modern technology

and you sit there
silent
ignoring the wrong

will you not speak up
and refuse to give your approval
to the wrongs of exploitation?

will you merely remain
quiet
and turn your head away from the wrong?

will you go on giving
your approval
as they exploit me with their cameras?

insider trading

there is a reason
why insider trading is
wrong

inside knowledge
gives unfair advantage
destabilizes the whole system

you can be sent up
for years and years
in a prison

all fear what will happen to the system
the potential for the wrong to be done
to them

fairness is safeguarded
with self interest in mind
and the weal of society

when i am watched
and my opponents are given unfair advantage
does it only effect me?

does not society become destabilized
law and order compromised
in the ethical wrong of watching?

every human being
understands why insider trading is wrong
and they understand what is done here is wrong

abused

i am abused
as i am monitored
against my will
and my life
laid bare for all to see

I am abused
as my weaknesses are examined
analyzed
with unauthorized video clips
studied to be used against me

i am abused
as my movements are anticipated
and my enemies
easily place themselves in my way
and try to make me fall

i am abused
by my enemies
who are intent on doing me evil
depleting me of my resources
and my potential

i am abused
as all stand by
and allow my enemies to place their players
as i walk blindly
into their traps

Watched

i am deprived

i am deprived
through the design
of the evil ones
who put traps in my course

when i am up for promotion
they sabotage my advancement
by using the camera
to see where they can place their traps

unfairly
i am deprived
of what should be mine
as surveillance cameras are used unjustly

to deplete me
to weaken me
to entrap me
it is so easy for them to do

for they see
where I go
they can place a trap
specially designed for me

they see where i am
what i read
what i say
where i am going

Watched

and they work to deprive
i am deprived
of what i can easily gain
what should be mine

as my enemies assail
using info they should not have
cameras they have no right to place
traps they cater to me where i am

i am deprived
as they try the best they can
using their resources
their means

with information
at their fingertips
as i walk blindly
into their trap

they set their trap easily
for they see
they know
using unfair information

and they are happy to use it against me
i am deprived
despite my skill
my achievement

for
my enemies unethically
place traps for me
a dozen times per day

Watched

hearts have become hardened

hearts have become hardened
to the wrong that go on here
as i am monitored against my will
my privacy taken away
a violation of human rights

will no one stand up and be ethical?
to say what is right
to uphold human rights
justice
will the evil manipulators win?

there is a grave injustice
a modern-day slavery of the will
depriving privacy
dehumanizing
objectifying a person

hearts have become hardened to the wrong
against the poorly treated person
who is deprived of his full potential
because the evil ones want their advantage
they have enslaved me using modern technology

all keep silent
as they manipulate
and try to fashion my life
to their advantage
hearts have become hardened like Pharaoh's heart

the evil game

an evil game is afloat
guess what
the watched
is thinking

bets
place your bets
what will he do
the watched

they do not see
the whole thing
stinks of violation
unethical!

a person has been
enslaved
like an object
his life deprived of privacy

he is objectified
only as the object
of an evil game
something to see

the evil game
continues
as people ignore the wrong
they throw him to the lions and watch

a teacher without pay

i am a teacher without pay
i impart wisdom
and knowledge
but they pay me not

they see through the cameras
that i did not even approve
and they breathe in
my hard-earned knowledge without pay

i labor to gain wisdom
and they steal my wisdom
without my permission
or approval

they just take lessons
and refuse to pay
they watch me
even when i frenetically object

i am a teacher without pay
for i teach
i always teach
and they are eager to learn

but they do not pay
and they feel no wrong in starving me
depriving me of my rightful wages
for my hard worked labors

Watched

easy to sabotage

it is easy
to sabotage
when you see
all that he does

focus on his weaknesses
ignore his strengths
highlight his weaknesses
use the formula to accentuate his weaknesses

sabotage his profession
sabotage his progress
sabotage his relationships
it's easy for they see where to set the traps

sabotage is the game
and it is an easy game to play
for the enemies
for they have evil access to cameras

they set them there
perhaps they asked someone to set them there
they may even have paid some
or tricked people into doing it

the cameras are set
unethically
and his enemies will use it
to sabotage his life

being watched

do you know
when you are watched?
how does that make you feel?

haven't you had the feeling
that you are being watched
even when no one was visible?

did you like that feeling?
how about when you were able to confirm it?
would you like to be watched constantly?

being followed
being watched
it affects the body and the mind

there is no respite
no personal space to retreat into
being always there to be watched

no freedom
no liberty
no rights intrinsically

do you like being watched?
to know that you can never get away
to a personal space of privacy?

About the Author

David Paul Folyant is an American poet living in Europe. David travels widely and thinks much about the future of humankind and his place in it.